Love Never Ends

To Joyce

With that Kind

of Love,

Flow

Florence Bishop Wolin

Florence Bishop Wolin

483 - 2211 home *
439 - 6399 cell
flowart@live.com

Love Never Ends

Published by Cornerstone Publishing, Inc., P.O. Box 2896, Virginia Beach, Virginia 23450.

Illustrations: Florence Bishop Wolin
Front cover design: Gann Graphics
Editing: Susan Bohannan

All Bible references are from the New King James Version unless otherwise noted.

First printing, 1997

Printed in the United States of America

DEDICATION

John 15:13 — Greater love has no man than this, that a man lay down his life for his friends. (RSV)

I dedicate this story to my mother, Florence Benham Bishop, who died March 23, 1981. I believe she laid down her life for Mary Jo, with great love.

IN APPRECIATION

To Jeanie Gilpin, Mary Jo's most steadfast friend. Jeanie is like a member of our family. She came to be with us in our darkest hours, from Wisconsin or Maine, or from wherever she was. She came to be with us.

As Mary Jo was dying, the nurse said of Jeanie and me, "Your two sisters are here." Jeanie said, "Close enough!"

I also wish to express my appreciation to Alberta Curtis and to Dr. Leon Cherry, whose encouragement led to this publication at this time.

Above all, to God be the glory!

FOREWORD

We often said to Mary Jo that she should write her story. She never wrote it on paper, but she wrote it on my heart. It is that story I seek to share with you. It is her story as seen through my eyes. In that sense, it will be inaccurate at times. I am not an objective observer. I am very much involved; I am her sister. Where my view would differ from hers, where my memory errs, I must admit, I give you my view of her story.

I am grateful to Mary Jo for sharing her life and death with me. I am grateful to friends for listening and caring. Above all I am thankful to God for "that kind of love."

It also has become apparent to me as I begin to write that I cannot write it all. It would take volumes! I pray that God will guide me to choose the words and thoughts to share.

Note from the author about the front cover:
  Daisies were Mary Jo's favorite flowers.
  Turquoise was my mother's favorite color.
  Butterflies symbolize Lupus and hope.

INTRODUCTION

I was privileged to meet Florence B. Wolin when I began teaching at Tidewater Detention Home, and it was immediately obvious that she was a compassionate individual who genuinely cared for the students! One year later, I can say that to know her is to know an angel in disguise. She is an inspiration to her students, staff, and fellow teachers, and she purposefully "flows" on out into the hedges and highways of life — seeking those who are in need of a kind word or a helping hand. She has even been known to provide a place of rest for the weary!

Flo has touched many lives with her warm smile, gentle hug, and words of encouragement. She is able to be such a blessing because God has endowed her with the greatest gift of all: the gift of love for and the willingness to share love with her fellow man!

— Alberta W. Curtis, art teacher
Tidewater Detention Home

The message is love.
God is love.
God loves.
Love is a gift from God
(unconditional, not dependent on circumstances).
Love last forever.
Love transcends time and space.
Love never ends.

Proceeds go to the Lupus Foundation.

I. Love Never Ends

I always thought we were close, friends as well as sisters. We shared a bedroom and a wardrobe, among other things. We were to become much closer before she died.

In 1968 I married against the wishes of my family. I feared I would lose their love forever. Mary Jo made a wooden plaque for me. On the front there were two girls, sisters I presumed, with their arms around each other. On the back it said, in Mary Jo's handwriting, "1 Corinthians 13:8a, With that kind of love, Mary Jo." I looked the verse up . . . "Love never ends." I cannot express what that meant to me, considering my marriage, against her wishes, my moving to Massachusetts from Virginia — both an emotional and physical separation. For eight years I lived with my husband in several homes away from Virginia and my family. In each home, that plaque found a special place. Mary Jo never liked it because it was rough and it buckled. It was not smooth or professional as some that she made later. I always told her, "I love it!" I told her that again her last day alive, in ICU.

1 Corinthians
13:8

*With that kind
of love . . .*

Mary Jo

II. A Bad Dream

I first learned of Mary Jo's illness when I was pregnant, in 1971. When my son Karl was born, in August 1971, Mary Jo was also in the hospital, ill. When Karl was a baby, Mary Jo was sick, then better, then sick, in and out of the hospital. She got engaged in the hospital, to David. He loved her anyway--sick or well! They planned their wedding from the hospital. It was a miracle to see her walk down the aisle March 26, 1972, radiant in love and joy — the picture of health!

But I had heard the word "Lupus" — "possibility of Lupus." The nurses who lived next door told me horror stories of later stages of Lupus. And yet when I asked Mary Jo, she said, "No, nephritis." It was confusing, difficult to diagnose. I tried to push it to the back of my mind.

In the fall of 1972, I moved to California, leaving Mary Jo in the hospital in Virginia, almost blind, with uncontrollable high blood pressure, and very frightened. It was her kidneys, we were told.

I went to California, and I had nightmares of her dying. The word "Lupus" gnawed at the back of my mind. I wrote to her doctor. He wouldn't discuss it. "You're not her next of kin."

I never again took Mary Jo for granted. I never again took health for granted. And Lupus has continued to gnaw at the back of my mind.

Mary Jo got better gradually, so much better we could almost forget. She took a lot of medicine, but she lived a fairly normal life.

We moved back from California to Virginia. I got divorced. My son Karl and I spent lots of time with Mary Jo and David after that, especially weekends.

I had been through a lot of feelings with my divorce, and I would share them with Mary Jo. She would be with

me and listen, but she rarely opened up and verbalized her own feelings. I wished she would be more open and expressed that to her several times. To further widen the gulf between us, she seemed uncomfortable when I would talk about God or Christ. I felt a sadness at the barriers I sensed between us. And yet, we were often together, as close as we could be.

In the fall of 1978, a rash on her face was diagnosed as "Lupus." By February she was sick again, the beginning of almost two years of unbelievable suffering. The dream was becoming a reality.

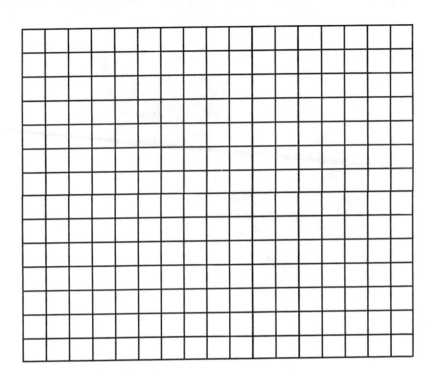

III. Counting the Squares

Mary Jo was in Portsmouth General Hospital from March until June, 1979. Her kidneys failed. They put a shunt in her leg, for "temporary" dialysis. "Temporary" became "endless." We went to the hospital daily — Mama spent most of the day there; Daddy and I came after work. Daily we saw her get worse. We saw her waste away to 75 pounds, lose her hair, lose the ability to feed herself, or speak, or move about. Lupus was destroying her lips and tongue. It attacked her heart, lungs, kidneys, bone marrow, brain — My God, when would it stop?! The doctors knew of nothing more to do. They seemed to have very little hope for her recovery.

When she first entered the hospital I told her I was asking people to pray for her. "Go ahead," she said, "but I don't have much faith in it." David had little faith in it then either, but we were desperate. We called everyone we knew who might pray. One night David asked me, "Isn't there anyone else?" We called a lady I had known in California who promised to send "pink light." "We'll take it!" David said, "we need all the help we can get!"

And we got a lot of help! People by the hundreds, maybe thousands, all over the country prayed, sent cards, and sent their loving support.

As Mary Jo grew physically weaker, I saw her grow spiritually stronger. She soon asked us to "visualize her as whole and well," a strange request when someone is dying. We spread her request. She refused to give up.

The Lupus was devastating, but it was no match for her determination. It went into remission at last, but it left its damage — kidneys that didn't work (dialysis needed three times a week), lungs badly damaged (oxygen needed), and a 75-pound body. With no muscle tone or ability to walk, she still used a walker, and we counted the blocks in the hospital room floor. Each block measured about one foot. It was progress when she could be rolled down the hall in the wheelchair, then to the lobby, then outside to see her pets, then down the sidewalk by the hospital! Progress was slow, but she never gave up.

How exciting it was when she came home from the hospital! Somehow we thought the struggle was over, the impossible goal reached. How devastating to face the irony of her reentering the hospital in just a few weeks, that it was not over. It went on and on and on and on . . .

And yet she kept on and on, she got better, gradually, slowly, with tremendous effort and determination.

IV. Counting the Blessings

I saw Mary Jo change. I saw us all change. You don't go through something like that without changing.

As the physical deteriorated, I saw the spiritual grow stronger and more beautiful. I saw and experienced joy in the midst of great pain and suffering. I remember Mary Jo's birthday, May 20, 1979, in Portsmouth General Hospital (her third consecutive month there). I arrived early, about 7:30 a.m., to surprise her and decorate her room. The family (Mama and Daddy, Karl, David, Mr. and Mrs. Hughes), shared the day in love and celebration. The hospital kitchen sent up a cake with candles. I was amazed at the radiant joy in her face, in her eyes! I continued to be amazed by that radiant glow of joy and love in Mary Jo, which sprung from within, not dependent on outer circumstances.

The secret, I believe, is love. The message over and over was love. There was so much love, or spiritual energy flowing towards Mary Jo from family and friends, and flowing from Mary Jo — it was amazing to me. I felt the pain and desperation, as we all did so many times. And yet in the midst of and alongside of the suffering, I experienced the love and joy. Because the love comes from God, and the love is God, the love is stronger!

At Mary Jo's memorial service, one of the ministers said, "Mary Jo learned to live and she learned to love." I agree with that. I believe that I also, as well as other family members and friends, learned much about loving and living from sharing with Mary Jo. I once told her that I felt almost guilty feeling glad for what I was learning from her illness and the sharing of it. She said not to feel guilty — that she was so glad that I, or anyone, could benefit from it. In fact, she decided that she had also benefited and was much happier than before she became sick. She would not trade it if she could. She said that she had once thought the most important thing in life was health, but now she realized that the most important thing was "love." She was happier because she had come to a place of love — love for self, love of God, love of others. She also was aware that she was loved by others and by God, but not for what she could do, because she could do physically very little. She was loved unconditionally, just as she was; and she knew it, and she accepted it. From this came peace and joy and strength.

I do not want to say that Mary Jo was always joyful. I saw Mary Jo fall down, physically, emotionally and spiritually. And I saw her stay down for a while. Then I saw her get up and go on. I remember one day when I had gone to pick her up from dialysis. When we got out of the car at Mama's house, she was weak and dizzy, so we simply sat down on the grass by the car. We stayed there for about 30 minutes, talking, enjoying a lovely day outdoors, and patting Cindy, a neighborhood dog. When Mary Jo was able, we got up and went in the house. It is a blessing to learn to relax and accept where we are now.

I saw Mary Jo angry — angry at life, angry at God. I heard her ask, "Why doesn't He either let me die or heal me?!" I heard her say, in despair, "He must be a cruel God. He must be punishing me." She asked the question, "Is He punishing me?" I saw her work through these difficult questions, to come gradually to a place of faith, trust and peace. She decided that God does not punish with illness; in fact, He does not cause illness. He does use illness for good in the lives of those it touches. She believed He had used her illness for good in her own life and in the lives of others. I believe Mary Jo's illness was used to draw many people closer together in love. I know it brought me closer to Mary Jo, to the rest of my family, and to many other people. It also brought me closer to an understanding of myself and closer to God. We learned to turn to God, because it was obvious

> # The only answer
> # I know is God.

that the burdens were too heavy for us to carry alone. I wrote these words for Mary Jo one Sunday afternoon, when she was ill and depressed, "The only answer I know is God." Months later, after she died, I found that same piece of paper on her dresser. It is still true for me.

Many times as I walked down the hall of the hospital, I would think, "I can't go in." I would pray for strength. It always came.

It is a blessing to learn to let go. I miss Mary Jo, but I have learned to let go. I said to her as she approached death, "It is all right to stay, and it is all right to go. Love never ends. We will always be together. Love transcends time and space. We will always be sisters. We will always be friends." The reason I can let go of someone I love is because love never ends. Relationships change; but in love, they do not end. My relationship with Mary Jo has changed, as she has gone into her new life; but it has not ended. Mary Jo has been victorious over her illness. She is not dead. She is alive and she is okay. I believe she loves us and is with us still, as we love her and are with her still. I believe death is not an ending, but a doorway to a new life. I rejoice with her, even as I cry for my earthly loss of her. Both are real — the sorrow and the joy. Above all else is love, and love never ends!

AFTERWARD

As I have reread my writing, I realize how much of Mary Jo's story I have left out. All I give you is some of my thoughts and feelings, as I reflect on her life and death, and their effect on me.

I wrote down my thoughts and feelings throughout the last few years. I want to include excerpts from these writings now, in closing.

SPRING

Lord,
You give to me . . .
Water in the deserts of my soul,
A way in the wilderness,
A silver moon to light my darkest night,
Sunshine piercing the clouds of my doubt,
Calm in the storms of my life,
A wellspring of joy from the depths of
    my sorrow.
A song of praise rising above my tears,
Healing for my pain,
Strength in my weakness,
Love overflowing from within —
I am thankful.

March 27

At Portsmouth General Hospital Mary Jo said, "The present moment is enough."

My thoughts: Lord, You are yet teaching me about loving and letting go, being still, patience, waiting, joy and peace from within, not dependent on outer circumstances. Soon after that, Mary Jo lost the ability to communicate by speech. She would attempt to speak, a few words would come with great difficulty. The effort was often too great for her weakened condition. She had to struggle to get her thoughts together. It was even too hard for her to follow our conversation. She expressed fear that the Lupus was reaching her brain. She was right.

I would go into her room and be quiet. There would be little conversation, yet there would be much communication.

April 9

Lord, You are teaching me
  the communication of silence,
  touching, eyes, nonverbal love.
Love is the strongest thing in the world.
You are the strongest! Your love is stronger.

You have answered my prayers. You have bound Mary Jo and me together in Your love. I feel loved and accepted by her at last. You have given her peace, joy, freedom and love — inner healing. Thank You for letting me be reassured that love is stronger, that You are stronger, that miracles are real and are happening. I see the inner healing already being accomplished. I am a part of it. I am accepted and loved.

She held my hand, she drew my body to hers. I heard her heart say, "Thank You, Father . . . thank You, Father." She touched me physically, emotionally, intellectually, spiritually. Thank You, Father. Greater is He that is in me . . .

May 9

I was driving to Portsmouth General Hospital with my son, Karl, and Mary Jo's small dog, Hilda, in my car. She was to be wheeled down to the sidewalk to see Hilda. Her therapist, Michael, had thought it would encourage her. She had not been outside in about two months, nor had she seen her pets. A storm came up on the way to the hospital. It poured, it thundered, lightening flashed! I thought to myself as I looked at the dark sky, "This is crazy! There is no way this will work." As I rounded the corner, I saw Mary Jo, in her wheelchair with her oxygen tank, and Michael, dry under a shelter, waiting to see Hilda.

I wrote: A shelter in the rain! Oh, ye of little faith. Why do I doubt You, Lord? Against all outer appearances, when I cannot see how it will possibly work out, You provide a way — a shelter in the rain.

May 20

Mary Jo's birthday. Be thankful for what is, instead of murmuring for what is not.

May 22

It is the inner, the unseen that lasts forever. It is the inner that matters.

June 3

Mary Jo went home from the hospital.

June 21

After Mary Jo reentered the hospital . . .
For the first time I have been experiencing what it is to turn off my feelings, because I cannot stay if I feel what I feel. I look out the window, I cook, I do anything but relate and feel.

July 6

Mary Jo came to my house! She ate dinner with us!

August 12

A prayer of release: I can release her into Your hands. Only You would I trust with the one I love so dearly, because I know You love her even more than I do. You can take care of her better than I can. I am so limited. You are not. I release her. My beloved, cherished one, into Your gentle, strong hands. Hold her in Your hands, Lord, ever gently, ever firmly, ever in love.

August 18

> We are here.
> Here is all we have.
> We are all we have.

September 3

> In the midst of our darkness, He is light.
> In the midst of our storms, He is peace.
> In the midst of our fears, He is calm.
> In the midst of our weakness, He is strength.
> In the midst of our doubts, He is wisdom.
> In the midst of our sorrow, He is joy.
> In the midst of our lives, He is Lord!

September 17

Lord, help.

There are no words.

And no one but You could possibly understand or help.

> Here is all I have.
> Right now, right here,
> In the middle of the mess
> That is my life,
> That is me.

If ever there is to be meaning, joy, peace, happiness —
I must find it here and now.

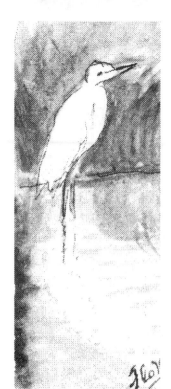

September 23, 24

A weekend at Chincoteague . . .
This weekend was a beautiful gift
from God . . .
Egrets, wild ponies, gulls
The sky spilling rain, gentle rain
The wind blowing, blowing
Time, hours of time . . .
Joy and peace and love to share
A wooded path, a nature trail,
paved for our wheelchair
Thank You, Father.

September 30

The only answer I know is God.
And God is enough.

October 28

Watch the leaves fall down
And praise the Lord!
Walk in the leaves on the ground
And praise the Lord!

For the Lord our God is a great God!
He lives forever.
And He is with us in all seasons.

Watch the leaves fall down
And rejoice!
Walk in the leaves on the ground
And rejoice!

Rejoice in their coming.
Rejoice in their going.
For the Lord our God is a great God!
He lives forever.
He is with us in our coming in and our going out,
Forevermore.

October, November

"Remission" — A Grace Period . . .

It may not last. Indeed, it will not last. It may all be gone tomorrow. It will certainly be gone someday. Does that make it any less valuable? No! Is value based on length of time? No! All we really have is the present moment. None of us has guarantees for tomorrow. Does that make today less meaningful, less to be enjoyed? We can't hold on. We must live in this moment and enjoy and let go. I can do that because God is the one certainty that will and does last. And He will take care of my tomorrow, too.

December 18

I go to Dialysis on Fridays
    for the gift I bring to Mama and to Mary Jo,
But most of all I go
    for the gifts I receive, for me.
I could get the gifts nowhere else,
    in no other way.
Karl is learning to appreciate life and health and love —
    so young (8 years old).
He is learning patience — so young.
I am learning to appreciate life and health and love —
    still young (35).

I am learning patience — still young.
I am learning to be and let be,
To accept without demanding.
I am thankful for the gifts.

December 22

I do not have the energy. I do not have the strength to
    face even
this one day, certainly not the next three or four! I want
    to open
myself more to You. Be the source of energy, of love,
    of strength,
for me today and forever.

December 24

Mary Jo gave me the greatest gift this morning on the
phone — the greatest gift is herself. She shared herself with
me. It really doesn't matter what happens later — now that
we have shared. We will always be sisters. We will always
be friends . . . We have a lot to be thankful for . . . It is a
beautiful Christmas! We are all together again, perhaps for
the last time.

December 25

Mary Jo, "a picture of health" — radiant! A miracle!

Tiny little budkin,
Bursting into bloom,
Don't you know
It isn't spring?
Nor will it be spring soon.

Don't you know it's time to sleep,
To hide from winter's cold,
All snug and warm
And safe from harm?
Why are you so bold?

You are so tender and so small.
You surely will not last.
A tiny flower such as you
Can't fight off winter's blast.

But does it really matter
If you will soon be gone?
You are beautiful today,
You laugh and sing and play.

And though I may wonder why,
I trust God's timing still.
Who am I to question
The timing of His will?

Tiny little budkin
Bloom, oh bloom today!
It's all we have,
Today that is,
And the timing, it is His!

WINTER

January 8

Dear Friends,

    As 1980 begins, I look back to 1979 and the many kindnesses each of you has shown to me. I would like to thank you for the cards, gifts, thoughts and prayers which helped me through some difficult times. Words cannot express the extent to which your love and support have helped me during the past months.

    Through each of you, God has performed countless miracles in my life during the past year. I look forward to seeing more of His miracles in 1980.

    For each of you, in 1980, I pray that the love you have given me will be returned and surround you throughout the year.

Sincerely,
Mary Jo Hughes

January 22

My mind is whirling, Lord,
Slow me down.
Wait and trust.
It is beyond my control.
I can pray, love, trust.
Bless her, Lord.
Hasn't she suffered enough?! Too much?!
My God, she suffers without complaint!
How can she keep on?
Lupus — I hate it! Won't it ever leave her alone?!
Go, Lupus, leave her alone! Can it be Your will for her?

No, I don't believe so. But I can believe You use it — even Lupus
You can use.
"Thou preparest a table before me in the presence of mine enemies."
In the presence of Lupus, You will take care of her.
In the midst of my fears, in the midst of my hurry,
In the midst of the mess, You take care of me, even now.
If she goes in the hospital tomorrow, I will trust You anyway.
The hospital is not the enemy. I should be thankful for the hospital.
It is not all over. We are not walking off into the sunset.
The problems never leave us. You are the God who is with us in the midst of the problems — right now.

January 27

The joy in living is the ability to see beauty and feel joy in the cold, in the rain, as well as in the warm sunshine. Unconditional joy — not dependent on circumstances. The source of joy is God.

February 13

A foot of snow!
It is beautiful, exciting, a miracle in Tidewater!
Mary Jo's lungs are healed and whole,
Mary Jo sledding and walking up a hill of snow,
Mary Jo laughing,
Mary Jo peaceful, open, trusting, praying, loving!
I do not question Your methods, Your will,
Your power,

Your timing anymore. You are my Lord. I bow
before You.
I am excited, joyful, rich, blessed. I am filled again and
again by You, Father.

March 5

With Mary Jo today —
I could do nothing.
I could say very little.
I could be with her.
"Be" is more important than do or say.

March 17

It is not over. It goes on and on. Perhaps that is what
makes release and letting go the only option. Let go —
release again
and again and again. The alternative (trying to handle
it alone)
is unthinkable.

May 25

Insecurity

There are many things
I do not know.
I do not know
If love will grow,
Or will you turn and run away?

I do not know
What lies ahead.
Tomorrow we
May all be dead.

I do not know what
Tests will show.
Will Karl be well,
Or_____?
Will Mary Jo_____

_____
_____?

I cannot even fill in these lines.
I cannot look to future times.
I trust in God
Who knows and cares,
And I'm thankful for the love He shares.

If I can't even ask the questions,
How could I hope
To have the answers?

May 26

Mary Jo and Karl united
   by salt-free diets,
      urine specimens,
         blood tests,
            changed life styles,
               limitations, prohibitions,
                  kidneys that don't work so well
                     anymore — at least right now!

My God, he's only eight!
And she is only 31!
United by youth.
How he loves her!
And how she loves him!
　　Both in love with David,
　　　　　And cared for by Grandma.
And Granddaddy can't make it "all right."

How hard it is for him.
How hard it is for me. PS: It's hard for him, too.

Waiting for the other shoe to fall . . .

June 1

This can't be real,
It is surely a dream,
I will wake up soon.

He can't be sick!
There must be some mistake!
He is only eight.
He has always been so healthy
All his life.
He can't be seriously sick.

Divorced,
My sister on dialysis,
My only son
Is sick.
This can't be real.

What's a nice girl like me
Doing in a place like this?

How are you getting along?
Bad.
Barely.
I won't lie.
I feel that way.
Don't ask
If you don't want to know.
I'm tired of coping,
Tired of being strong.
I'm tired
Of taking care of others.
I give up.
I want so much
For someone
To take care of me.
Won't somebody call,
Reach out to me.
I am passive,
So tied up in my pain,
Immobilized.
There are those who do care
I could call. I am glad,
And yet
I am alone
In my pain.
Okay. I'll be alone.
I don't need you.
Right now
I'll be alone.
I'll hide behind my walls
In my pain.

June 5

I feel like
I have been clobbered,
Run over,
Beaten down
Beyond belief.
It is like a bad dream
Repeating itself
Again.
Enough is enough!
I am tired of it!

It is as if I observe
Myself
Going through motions.
Numb
Beyond believing.
This can't be real.
It is a bad dream
Repeating itself
Again.
Biopsy,
Steroid drugs,
24 hour urine
Tests, tests, tests, wait and know nothing,
And yet it is a beautiful day.

July 9

Still waiting . . . My times are in Your hands.
I make decisions, I make plans . . . in futility . . .
   In faith . . .
All can change instantly.

I do not know what to do or how.
Please remake me and my plans. Thy will be done.
We wait . . .
   In futility or in faith?

I am thankful that he feels so well.
He looks well.
I am thankful that she is happy.
We wait . . .
   In frustration and fear?
Or in thankfulness and faith?

July 23

I am thankful for the nurses and doctors
Who rock, who cuddle, who kid, who play,
Who take the time,
As well as the vital signs.
We all surely die without love.
With love we may get well.

July 23

Biopsy —
What an ugly word.
Dr. Pryor is a gentle, loving man.
He likes Karl.
Surely he would not do an ugly, cruel thing to Karl.
I must be looking at it wrong.
Who is the enemy?
Surely not Dr. Pryor or his biopsy.
Who do we fight? Disease . . . too vague.
A war with no enemy.

At MCV, Kidney Transplant Unit, Nephrectomy . . .

Mary Jo — peaceful, radiant — eyes sparkling, alive and in love. Thy will be done.

Mary Jo said: Whether we live or whether we die, let us love. Love is more important than anything else, even physical health. I would rather be sick and loved and loving than well and alone without love.

The message is love.

God is love.

God loves.

Love is a gift from God (unconditional — not dependent on circumstances).

I have found joy in today!
Love in the suffering
Radiance in Mary Jo's face,
Sparkle in her eyes.
Love overflowing!
Water in the desert.
I am amazed and excited!
Thank You, Father.
I am rich and blessed.
My cup overflows with love.

July 30, 31

What a way to learn patience — live it — moment by moment in Dialysis, on the Transplant Unit, lying still with both arms stilled by tubes. Learn patience and letting go. Let go of control — there is no controlling what happens.

There is a lot of time. Time moves slowly. Messages on be and being, less to do, more to be.

August 9

As I become aware
That I can do nothing for you,
I am free to be me
And be with you.
For the greatest gift
Is simply just to be with.

September

The roses are a gift,
    A gift to me,
    A gift to share.

The Giver of the roses
    Sent one to tend them,
Tenderly, quietly, gently,
    In the fullness of time.

In the fullness of time . . .
    One day . . .
    The spider is gone.

Life does not end.
    Life changes,
Life goes on . . .
    In the fullness of time.

September 25 to November 16

Mary Jo at MCV — Kidney Transplant Unit
Excitement! Amazement! Disbelief! Joy! Hope!
Reasons to pray — platelets, urine . . .
Tonight it rains!
I don't want to hear

That the rain is too late.
I don't want to hear
It isn't enough.
I don't want to hear that the rain won't last.
Tonight it rains!
It is enough
To enjoy
The rain
Tonight.

A beautiful dream achieved turns sour. A cruel joke. The kidney works, and the mind and intestines go now. My God, how much can she suffer? How much can we suffer? No more.

We celebrate her new life and ours. And yet we mourn the loss of Mary Jo physically in our lives.

November 1

At MCV . . .

I am alone.
I am to do nothing.
I am alone with God.
Is there no one else?
No, there is no one else.
What am I to do?
Nothing, My child.
You are My child, as is Mary Jo.
I take care of My children.
You need do nothing.
That is the secret.
Love is eternal,
Love never ends,

Love transcends time and space . . .

I wish I could save her from more suffering and pain.
I am glad I do not have such power
   To decide for another soul.
Who am I to presume that I know
   What is best for her?
Thy will be done.

November 3, 4

I say to Mary Jo:
It is okay to leave.
It is okay to stay.
Love lasts forever.
Love transcends time and space.
Love never ends.

November 5

When I look at the bedspread, I feel guilty giving up. How did she ever have the courage to buy that bedspread for a home she might never see again?

I used to have hope, too.

I remember buying the clothes for her . . . I almost returned them once . . . but I kept them as a pledge of faith . . . And she lived to wear them and to use the bedspread. Or was that living? I have no more faith. I'm tired of believing. I give up.

If You want me to have faith, You'll have to supply it, Lord. I fear Mary Jo is quitting, too. If You want her to get well, You'll have to do it.

We're all tired, Lord. It's up to You.

Do what You want, but You do it!

. . . It breaks my heart
　　　To see Mama and Daddy
　　　　　Keep on trying,
　　　　　　Keep on hoping,
　　　　　　　Keep on smiling
　　　　　　　　Keep on —
　　　　　　How do they do it?
Isn't there any end?
　　No, there's no end —
　　　　Only changes,
　　　　　　No destination.
　　　　　　　It's all a process.

November 7

More lessons in love not tied to response.
If I can't leave with my body,
I'll leave with my mind.
Drugs to alter her mind?
Won't anyone let her choose to die?
Drugs, surgery, machines
　　maintain life and destroy and twist it.
Let her be! Enough is enough!
I said, "It's okay to leave."
She did, in the only way she could.

I miss you,
　　and it's okay to leave.

November 8

She is choosing to leave the only way she can. I ask myself, "Is she leaving temporarily or permanently?" The answer for me is temporarily. We are one in God's Spirit for eternity.

When I am ready to die,
I won't go to MCV.
They do too good a job of preserving life,
Or is it life?
This is life! Here, now.
Here, where birds bathe freely,
And squirrels scurry and scamper,
And leaves fall to earth
When they are ready to die
And return to the earth
To be born again
In the gentle flow of life . . .

Man and his machines
Interrupt life,
    Interfere with life.
In trying to make life better
We twist and destroy
    the natural flow of life.
We fix one thing
    And destroy another.

A fuzzy stick from Wisconsin,
A stuffed cat turns upside down,
We smile. We laugh.
We begin again to hope.

November 16

No more tubes.

November 18

Mary Jo's Memorial Service . . .

Mary Jo, I love you!
Go out in Joy,
Leaves falling.
Rain, sunshine, wind, cold, warmth, all of nature says
"Yes." This is an important day! A day of love and loss. A
day of joy and sorrow. A day of fear and peace. It is raining
and the sun is shining. Both are true, not either . . . or.

November 28

They say my car is "totaled,"
Well, I feel "totaled" too.
They say my car is repairable,
I guess I'm repairable, too.
It costs a lot to repair my car,
but it's worth it to me because I love my car.
It costs a lot to repair me,
but it's worth it to God, because He loves me.

Waiting for the other shoe to fall . . .

My God,
    When I look at that urine,
    I fear it isn't over yet.
My God,

I'm tired of sickness and pain,
And I haven't even been sick yet!

But I've known pain of the spirit,
Pain of the soul that cares
For a sister, or a son
who is sick.

Oh, my God!
When will the sickness end?!

December 7

(at the Green's Farm)

Mary Jo —

Whenever I see a marsh
I shall think of you,
Silent beauty
Golden now,
Afire with setting sun.
Quietly, unobtrusively,
radiantly aglow,
You taught me a lot about marshes
and silence.
You shared the beauty of marshes.
You shared the beauty of silence.
You share the beauty of silence still.
P.S. And I miss you.

December 11

> We can say the "if only's"
> Until we are blue in the face,
> And it doesn't change a thing.
> Just accept what is,
>   As it is.

December 12

It was a beautiful and awful day. Both are true. It was beautiful and ugly. Both are true. The ugliness does not negate the beauty. The anger does not negate the love. The sickness does not negate the health. Death does not negate life. Both simply are, side by side, often mixed simultaneously. It is life.

A "real" Messiah — surely if God is all powerful, He could have sent a Messiah to save the world — to abolish all pain, sorrow, hunger, sickness, death, injustice. Instead, He sent a Messiah to show us how to live with these things--to live as humans and to die as humans. He spoke to us about our inner selves, the spiritual peace in the midst of the storm. It is true that He did calm one storm at least, but He did not abolish all storms. He did heal some sickness and raised one man from the dead. But He did not abolish all sickness and death.

"Do not lay up for yourselves treasures on earth, where moth and rust destroy and where thieves break in and steal" (Matthew 6:19). It is the spirit that really matters! It is the spirit of man that the Messiah was sent to save.

December 24, 25

More than any other night,
Christmas Eve was her night.
To me, for me,
Christmas Eve is forever
Interlocked in my memory
With Mary Jo.
   As children,
      As adults,
         We have shared so many Christmas Eves.

Are You sure, Lord,
That it was supposed to end like this?
Are You sure
   It wouldn't have been better another way?

41

Who am I to question?
I am overwhelmed.
I give up.
He shall reign forever and ever.
He is the only answer I know,
The only reason I know to rejoice,
Rejoice anyway.
Celebrate Christmas anyway.

Christmas came anyway,
Without Mary Jo.
I never put my faith in things.
I have put faith in people.
I have seen people going and gone,
Gone, and yet still here (never gone in spirit and in love).
People I love going and gone . . .
  When? Where? How? Why? Who knows?!
I give up.
Put faith in God.
And He shall reign forever and ever.

I am thankful for the blessings of death, and yet I miss
you. We can't go to Williamsburg at Christmas this year. I
mourn your absence here as I celebrate your new life.

NEW YEAR

January 1

May 1981 be a better year than 1980! I'll drink to that!

Was 1980 such a terrible year? Yes! It was damn tough! We went to hell and back as a family, with sickness and pain and suffering — hospitals — doctors —wait and know nothing — uncertainties — build up hopes, see them crash down into the pits! Auto accidents — anything can go instantly. Oh my God, it has felt like hell!

And yet it has been beautiful. Tears flowing free, friends that care and share, hands to hold and support one another on the way to hell and back. The radiance of love and joy in the midst of pain and suffering. Love is triumphant even in death. Friends that are giving to me when I cannot even ask, when I have nothing to give in return. God, in the midst of the storm, You have always been with us, giving us joy in the midst of sorrow, peace in the midst of turmoil, faith in the midst of fear, strength in the midst of weakness, love overflowing! You, our God, have not deserted or failed us. Any year with You, Oh God, is a beautiful year. I commit this new year unto You, Oh Lord. May it be Your year and lived in Your will and Your way. I do not pray for a year without storms — I pray for a year with You, Oh my Father. I love You anyway.

February 4

Yes, let me remind myself of the learnings now,

Now that I miss her, now when I hear the pain in Mama's voice,

"The estate of Mary Jo Hughes" — She really is dead.

Never again in this lifetime will I see her.

The pain is real and it hurts.

I am a survivor.
I have stumbled away from a holocaust,
Dazed, stunned beyond belief,
Grateful to be alive,
Grateful to be left alone.

I am numb, dazed by the
    suffering I knew,
The pain, the feelings begin
    to seep through.
They will be a long time
    coming into view.

March 1

I am witness to a miracle,
A miracle of love and joy
    in the midst of pain and suffering.
I am grateful to have shared,
    to have been a part of it.
I am amazed beyond belief
    at the beauty of a human soul
            in the face of destruction
                of the human body.
The love, the joy begin to seep through.
They will be a long time
    coming into view.

April 28

As I see it now:

How strange a thing is perspective; we thought 1980 was a terrible year. And yet this morning as I spray my rose bushes for bugs, I remember fondly the "Rose Garden Spider" and I wish for her protective presence. I remember the year of "reprieve" with Mary Jo growing stronger and more loving. I remember Mama's last year. I remember shared times with Norm, even holidays and very special days. All are gone now. What a gift was 1980, as I see it now.

May 15

At last, silence. I hear wind in the trees, what a blessed sound. The rose garden spider's baby is in my roses. I see her grow daily, to become like her mother in miniature — so very tiny, black with teeny yellow stripes. I said, "Welcome! I am glad you are here. I have hoped you would come. I knew your mother well. Welcome to my rose garden." What a blessing and gift.

Since I have only now, I choose carefully how I will spend it.

Now is a time to be still, to consolidate, to regroup, to renew. It is not a time to reach out, to extend. I am still.

FIFTEEN YEARS LATER

Fifteen years later, I am more convinced that love never ends. Even though I still miss my sister and my parents on the physical plane, I do feel their love and presence spiritually.

Since 1981, I have consolidated, regrouped and renewed. I have also risked reaching out to many others who suffer. Because I have experienced my own pain and survived, with God's help and guidance, I have been able to encourage other suffering souls.

I believe God has called me to share His unconditional love with His troubled children, especially the emotionally disturbed and incarcerated. In my work as a teacher at Tidewater Detention Home, I am able to bring God's light and love into the darkness. God enables me to love His children, who are victims and perpetrators of violence.

Through my own sorrow and pain, God has prepared me to face even death unafraid. "Though I walk through the valley of the shadow of death, I will fear no evil; You are with me" (Psalm 23:4).

Fifteen years later, God is still the only answer I know, and I know that God's love never ends.